EMOTIONAL INTELLIGENCE

EMOTIONAL INTELLIGENCE

Mastering Relationships and Success

SERAPHINA BLAKE

QuillQuest Publishers

CONTENTS

CHAPTER 1

Introduction

There are four domains of emotional intelligence. The first domain, perceiving emotions, consists of skills in recognizing how others feel. The second domain, using emotions, refers to appropriately expressing how we feel. The third domain, understanding emotions, includes skills in recognizing how others feel, predicting future emotions, and using this information to make decisions. The fourth domain, managing emotions, involves dealing with emotions expressed by ourselves and others. Each domain encompasses a unique set of skills that can be measured with performance-based tests. The broader the span and variety of tests used to measure skills within those domains, the less "contaminated" learning-specific knowledge of the measure, and therefore, the more likely that domain skills are genuinely addressed in training. The intellectual history behind this claim comes from general trainability evidence for diverse abilities.

Emotional intelligence involves a set of skills that help us perceive, understand, express, reason with, and manage emotions in ourselves and others. In life and especially in business, it is more than just important - it determines our success. It has been recognized as a great aid in decision making, healthcare, and many life fields. Businesses and organizations are catching on and are using emotional intelligence as part of their hiring and promotion processes. Some of the most impactful accomplishments can only occur when someone has high levels of emotional intelligence. However, a common misconception is that emotional intelligence is inherent and cannot be developed. The field of cognitive training has demonstrated that the brain is far more malleable than previously thought, and whether intelligence or memory can be improved by training through an approach termed deliberate practice that involves carefully structured exercises. Similarly, emotional intelligence can also be improved through emotional skills training that provides opportunities for deliberate practice.

CHAPTER 2

Understanding Emotional Intelligence

The emotional world is much more complex than it might seem at first glance. Emotions are multicausal, that is, there are several factors that cause them, and experience causes the exact feeling of happiness, anger or sadness that cannot be exactly the same as that of the rest of the people. We can try to understand the reactions of the people, to put ourselves in their place, but even if we deduce what they might be feeling, how we can avoid it is a subject that exceeds our capacities of understanding, an unsolved mystery. The fact that we humans are the only species capable of recognizing our own emotions and the feelings of others with all their complexity does not help to solve the problems. Today we live too dependent on the logical side, forgetful of the emotional side. We have been educated with the idea that the expression of our emotions should be minutely controlled and, at best, overlooked. Even though diving into emotions can help a better understanding of the person we are communicating with, the fact is that no one ever tells us that appalling others, our saying what we think or expressing our fears and insecurities are the only medium that can save us from the most difficult situations. It is about knowing and managing our emotions.

What's emotional intelligence? In the last two decades, the scientific interest in emotional processes has given rise to the field of investigation known as emotional intelligence. Although a lot of concepts have been given, the idea of EI can be summarized as a set of emotional skills. It is this set of abilities that enable us to play with others in the emotional arena, to relate to others and to interact with them. As a starting point to understand the enormous scope of the concept, and the multiple translations that can be found to define it, you could explain that EI is "the ability to recognize and understand our own feelings and those of others and the ability to manage emotions and their proper scope".

CHAPTER 3

Developing Self-Awareness

Additionally, develop the habit to reflect on your feelings and thoughts. Introspection is the first step to self-awareness. Frequent introspection helps you develop the observant muscle in your brain that observes the intentions, goals, and values driving your reactions. Finally, it is necessary to master your self-control. At times, your reflexes may lead your actions and thoughts in a biased way not aligned with your true intentions. To support these efforts, remove external distractions and regulate the emotions generated from within. Understanding how to recognize and manage emotion is the essence of self-awareness. Do it for yourself, to meet your needs and enable your desires. Understand your emotions to harness their energy to think and behave the way you need to not just to appear emotionally intelligent but to become emotionally intelligent.

Chapter 3. Developing Self-Awareness. The first step to developing emotional intelligence is to realize the extent to which your mind can work against you. Rather than seeing the world as it is, we often see the world through how we are, biased by our beliefs and interpretations of events. Next, develop self-awareness, which gives you the objectivity to recognize that you are feeling an emotion. Begin to observe the thoughts that drive those feelings. You have to develop the self-awareness to observe or watch what your mind tells you to do. By growing your awareness, you can then choose the response you will take. This choice is limited by your awareness so you must continue to grow your acute observation and reflection continually.

CHAPTER 4

Enhancing
Self-Management Skills

Self-management, commonly known as self-regulation by some professionals, is your ability to use emotions in the service of a goal. This means choosing how you respond to an emotion, instead of automatically or reflexively reacting. The capacity to act in control of your emotions has what it takes to change how you bring yourself to work. How you think and feel about any situation, and how you interact with others, will depend mainly on your state of mind. This is why it's crucial to ensure you're constantly maintaining an adept emotional condition to determine how you come across to your team members, coworkers, and clients. The way you present yourself at all times directly affects your relationships, and this is what it boils down to every time it's thought of enhancing your self-awareness skill.

By exercising self-management skills, you're able to manifest self-control that can result in what is naturally regarded as self-empowerment. It can help foster self-discipline that carries a positive effect in every aspect of your personal and professional lives. The five abilities that a person with high self-management knows how to use easily are self-control, transparency, adaptability, initiative, and optimism. It's crucial to learn how to manage our emotions when working with a team or with a difficult coworker. Maintaining an ideal emotional state requires work, but it's one of the many achievements you can expect from enhancing your self-management abilities.

CHAPTER 5

Cultivating Empathy

If you want to understand a person, look deeply into your heart. Find out what hurts it, and that is what hurts the most. When you understand and feel someone's pain and joy as if they were your own, and when you do not inflict your more new, creative ideas but alternatively support or gently help them to bring what was hidden within them into existence, you are practicing empathy. As many of us know, empathy can't be learned from a book. However, there are practices we can do to help us become more mindful, aware, and emotionally connected. Understanding the cause and effects of these practices allows us to see the world more deeply from each other's shoes and helps us develop the mind of wisdom and compassion. This too isn't just a new, more perfect replacement for our old habits but sends a place our relationships, careers, and personal lives can quite possibly reach unexpected, deeper levels through pain and loss. Understanding the cause and effects of these practices allows us to see the world more deeply from each other's shoes and helps us to meet others where they currently are, rather than demanding that they be our personal substitutes or hand us the grains. This place their relationships, careers, and personal lives can be modified in ways that create a more profound human connection.

Empathy is the single most important ingredient in the recipe for successful personal relationships. It is the power of meaningful, ceaseless recognition that we really need to understand each other. Practicing the art of empathy – getting in tune with your deepest feelings – is one of the keys to living a happy and successful life. For empathy allows you to see the colors of the world in a much clearer light, free of bias and judgment, free of meanness.

CHAPTER 6

Improving Social Skills

Yoga master Paramahansa Yogananda observed: "If you cannot get along with yourself, weak will be your power to get along with others. Man is his own severest critic. It is easy to look into the faults of others and point them out, but difficult to see one's own limitations, hence the practice of hammering away our character flaws and weaknesses is a matter that is entirely between ourselves and our Maker." Hammering away character flaws and weaknesses? That's what yoga is all about. The paradox of developing emotional intelligence, according to the authors of "Emotional Intelligence," is that self-control, zeal, persistence, and a mastery of ethical behavior emerge as potentialities of success (as does an improvement in the cultivation of the social graces of persuasion), once social skills are affirmed.

Research in the area of emotional intelligence shows that those with high emotional intelligence are more capable of leading people and making good decisions. Why? In part, because emotional intelligence is largely a social skill and social skills are more important than ever in the information age. In the industrial age, people generally worked in isolation and needed only technical skills such as literacy and number skills. But increasingly, the industrial age is giving way to the information age wherein the social skills, such as empathy, cooperation, and the ability to relate emotionally with others, are becoming more important. The social intelligence skills predicted which workers would be the most effective in a company more than people's mental abilities.

CHAPTER 7

Building Stronger Relationships

There is one problem: this blueprint for relating is four thousand years old. Then, millennia ago, an event turned our family home into a single room where we had to weave our lives together much more closely. We moved from operating as separate, like islands bobbing up and down in a communal sea, to coordinating our emotional states much more closely and often than any of us had asked for or liked. Strangers grew into a crowd, and singles melted into couples. We spent much of our personal and communal life negotiating our emotional terrain. This shift from the anonymity of the city to the invisibility of the web has made matters even more complicated. Even before the so-called Information Technology revolution occurred, 99.999% of what we were perceiving emotionally was processed wordlessly. As the big shift occurred and successfully reduced the mental isolation of many a working-at-home techie, new mental boundaries had to be constructed to limit emotional overload and intrusion because now the demands of many others were piped directly into our brain. What is the collective impact of reducing face-to-face interaction while increasing emotional traffic? We predict considerably less focus on the good of the whole —the worrying global implications include everything from ecological conservation to terrorism prevention—as people start and seek to operate in smaller groups, often single-sex like their ancient ancestors. While the net has created a shared code of behavior, we have already seen pockets of public emotion. This trend will continue in the coming years as net denizens strive to reformulate an ambiguous shared code of what it now means to be human in this kind of world and in an ever-increasingly heart-stopping reality.

Our emotionally intelligent ancestors lived in small, closely bonded groups, with a set of customs and rituals and a shared emotional world. This was not always peaceful or pleasant, but it always involved a heightened awareness of and a tolerance for diverse emotional realities. And so it was that we charted our first maps for relating. These maps were loaded onto the navigational systems of our species; now, although setting off on very different voyages, many of us are still working from this original blueprint for effective relatedness.

CHAPTER 8

Emotional Intelligence in the Workplace

According to the latest news from Business News Daily, emotional intelligence (EI) is defined as "the ability to identify and manage one's own emotions, as well as the emotions of others. Intelligence plays a critical role in how successful an individual will be in the workplace as well as in their personal life. The business world is a highly analytic, logical, and data-driven culture, and those who prefer to think intellectually and ignore their emotions will often be left behind. However, forgetting or ignoring this important area can lead to disasters in professional relationships. As you might notice, there is a tendency to value emotional intelligence. Rogers and colleagues conducted a research study with 400 participants and attributed 58.9% of job changes to difficulties in handling emotions and not learning from critical feedback, while only 19% of job changes were contributed to skills and knowledge. This could be the hard material evidence to prove that EI does have a positive predictive competency in the workplace.

Now, a personal perspective on the implications of emotional intelligence in the workplace. The literature and research reviewed here are abundant, and the implications extend across all disciplines and aspects in business. In HR, we are used to seeing the EQ-I being able to predict 69% in successful job performance, in addition to other important skills such as cognitive ability and relevant work experience. For the same reason, the EQ-I is "almost" considered as "a standard" when assessing competences. A good reason is that it explains around 26% variance in the competency measure.

CHAPTER 9

Managing Conflict Effectively

The first "technique" for managing anger is to increase pleasure and eliminate displeasure in everyday activities. When people are less often in unpleasant or disturbing states, they are less prone to anger or other negative emotions. Next, they improve how they physically respond to the inevitable little unpleasant moments, to keep these minor irritations from piling up and compounding into full-blown anger. Another habit improvement that some people develop is recognizing when they make any of several types of anger-linked misinterpretations and other confusions, and correcting for this as well as isolating the situations in which emotions naturally arise. A third strategy for anger control is developing what are known as aggressive thought patterns, positive ways of thinking that lead not just to suppression or neutralization of anger. They lead to a more constructive problem-solving process as well as a more motivating outcome.

One of the most controversial emotions in the work setting is anger. It is considered controversial because its expression is generally deemed unacceptable. Nevertheless, there is no use in pretending that people do not get angry in the work context. And, whether we acknowledge their existence and influence, anger and other negative feelings are profoundly influential. All kinds of behaviors occur that are destructive to the work environment, harmful to the target of the anger (and to the person experiencing the anger), and a detriment to task completion. People get angry because they misinterpret situations, associate unrelated or past issues with events at hand, have basic differences in concepts or philosophies, view the context from different perspectives, or just are having a bad day.

CHAPTER 10

Emotional Intelligence and Leadership

Leadership development since the end of the Second World War was more closely related to the work of the behavioral school, with the manager being considered under the 'scientific model' as a mechanic in its human model, in the General Philosopher. The modern view of leadership takes the propensity to marry individual intelligence - IQ and abstract/technical rationality - with the emotional dimension. Since the first studies in the 1980s, the importance of emotional intelligence as an essential ability for effective leadership versus the exercise of power has been established. According to this study, emotional intelligence has a lot to contribute to the leadership and management function in different organizations regardless of their nature, complexity, and size, and thus financial results are the necessary consequence of emotional intelligence.

In recent years, there has been a sharp rise in books, articles, and seminars for managers and executives who are trying to improve the quality of their leadership. The effectiveness of management and the powerful impact on the bottom line account for this rising phenomenon. The corporate world and its protagonists, as clairvoyant, began to understand the great importance of the emotional side or emotional intelligence as the main attribute of leadership and, consequently, of real and unforgettable leaders. The driver of both business success and the improvement of the harmonious living of societies. This global 'movement' is now so fully integrated that colleges and universities have started to offer leadership programs, with the same magnitude as business courses were offered. And, on the other hand, psychologists have programs to teach emotional intelligence to future administrators.

CHAPTER 11

Emotional Intelligence and Personal Success

People's professional growth is highly dependent on peers. Often, employees cap performance levels, either because they do not feel respected or they feel that their voice is not listened to. Professionals of today's world receive an enormous amount of information on a daily basis and feel a vortex of sensations spiral around them. To be successful requires focusing not just on cognitive aspects, but also on emotional, spiritual, and physical aspects. These are factors that influence the way our brain is able to elicit maximum performance from the mind, body, and spirit. If people are not able to exploit situations with a high degree of stress, they are not emotionally intelligent. Maintaining relationships with important people can determine success. A good reputation, or maintaining one, is a means for securing trust and respect in the long term.

Extensive study and research has shown that EI is pivotal for personal success. There are a number of indicators that reflect a high EI: optimism, well-being, openness, achievement drive, and initiative. Severe stress disintegrates the hippocampuses of the brain, impeding people's learning, critical thinking, decision making, and cognitive flexibility ability, which are all determinants of career success. In good times, an employee who sings a company's praises is less productive than one who criticizes it. However, in difficult times, it is just as important in terms of the business's health. 'Yes-men' are the death of businesses. Good management is based on the collaboration between staff members. A person with emotional intelligence will not just maintain his/her performance, but it will improve over time. Extensive research has shown that people are not often gifted individuals, but talented groups. Empathy and use of all the senses are paramount to catalyze a group's capacity for collective intelligence.

CHAPTER 12

Conclusion

Emotional intelligence and academic aptitude abilities are doubtless similar. It seems strange that the phrase is more appealing than the word, so that rather than speak of emotional ability we say "emotional intelligence". But we can still ponder why intelligence is associated with life skills that emerge later on the developmental timescale and whether that is necessary. Perhaps we do not need a broader notion of intelligence, nor emotional intelligence for that matter. And yet, to account for eventualities, we could remind ourselves of why the concept was generated in the first place. It was a matter of training needs - of wanting a better understanding of people's likely trajectories in dealing with problems of everyday life and of wanting to enhance them.

This brief article offers two main conclusions. The use of the term "intelligence" to mean a broader set of abilities over and above those of traditional understanding has generated a great deal of controversy and a proliferation of claims, all the way from qualifications to flashes of insight. It turns out that we need not fear the widening implications of intelligence, so long as we remember that attention to particular purposes is essential. In certain respects, putting the term front and center in our field was disingenuous. But if we can assimilate and exploit the rich resources and interconnections of the various research areas, we should not be afraid to be as ambitious as we account of the range and nature of the abilities needed for intelligently managing life without assuming that all possible abilities or forms of knowledge are of equal importance to all problems or exist in equal measures within a single person.